Can You Hear Me?
-I am not listening-

Heather Sawyer

ISBN:
ISBN-13: 978-0692063804

DEDICATION

THE PROCESS IS WHAT PUSHED ME AWAY, BUT IT IS ALSO WHAT BROUGHT ME BACK. I COULD SAY IT WAS COUNTLESS CUPS OF COFFEE ON WEDNESDAYS, FAMILY DINNERS, BREWERY TRIPS AND GIGGLES, BUT THAT WOULD BE FALSE. I NEEDED TO SIMPLY STOP LOOKING AND MOVE FORWARD, INCOMPLETE OR NOT.

CONTENTS

ACKNOWLEDGMENTS

Sheldon for understanding and letting me be me and still loving me
Grace for friendship, laughter, tears and a whole bunch of crazy
Sandy for helping me find some of the answers, even the ones I
didn't want to find
Jodi for her honesty and friendship
Piper for a second chance because everyone deserves one
Shortcake for reminding me that I love words
Sweet tooth and Curly for their unconditional love

I may not always see the bigger picture, but I am so very lucky to have so
many people to help me forge a path.

Ignorance
&
Shame

Take a Walk With Me
an
Introduction of Sorts

When I first sat down to write this memoir of sorts I had no idea what this truly meant or where to start. I knew I needed to start with one memory and go from there. But the concept of delving into multiple memories was not something I really wanted to do, especially if they involved her, I missed her. I wanted to sit back and let the embers fade, it seemed like the easiest solution. Without a breathe of oxygen they would fizzle and I would simply move on as if nothing had ever happened. It was what I wanted to do, but the more I tried to ignore what I was thinking, the more it assaulted my brain, so I sat down and put the words to paper. I didn't want to, but I did and in doing so I realized that there are parts of our lives that are meant to be looked at and others that are not.

I put a fan to the embers cautiously, but a fire erupted anyway and the thoughts ravaged me faster than I was prepared for. I didn't want to face them, but the words flooded my brain. Then the memories were there in front of me, so I let them in. I uncharacteristically let them in, so I began with what I thought was a simple word: Love.

Love is a funny thing. According to the dictionary it means to have affection for, but what does that really mean? Affection is a vague term that can be applied to many things. I mean who doesn't have affection for purses and shoes, right? Love on the other hand is something that should be reserved for family, friends and lovers.

With that in mind, I am not sure what it is that I want out of this journey I am on. It has been more difficult than I imagined it would be. The initial thoughts come so easily, but then they morph and change, complicating the story. I have always considered her part of my life, family really, even when she wasn't. In many ways I had made a place for her in me and I wasn't sure what that meant, but now as I sort through the details of it all, I wonder if maybe I was wrong. Wrong to have let her in even though I wanted to. She often pushed me to do things that I would not have the courage to do on my own because they would seem unimportant without her. With that said, I now find myself questioning my own instincts, unsure of what I want out of life. I thought by writing about things, that maybe, just maybe I would come to a different conclusion, but I am not sure I have. I see the choices that I made, the ones I continue to make, the feelings that I had and refused to accept or even process and I am left wondering, was it worth it? Was that simple word, love, really so simple after all?

May
7:00 PM

Red wine stains everything. Rugs, clothing, people, have all fallen into the spell of the forbidden grapes and they always come back for more. I surely did and I am still scrubbing.

It starts innocently, dancing, teasing, that's what best friends do right? I think so, but copious amounts of red wine breeds danger. I should know, I have been here before, just not with her. She is different.

There were others, toys to amuse myself between classes and immature men, none of them were her. We are friends and I love her. There I said it, I love her. I know, I know its bad, but I am not in love with her. I simply love her more than my other friends, maybe more than I care to mention and that will always terrify me.

She knows everything there is to know about me and she still supports me, go figure. We battle for each other and always step up to catch each other when things fall apart. Am I going to ruin that? I don't really know, but I can confidently say that the answer to that question does not reside at the bottom of my wine glass regardless of how long I look for it there.

Kryptonite

-I can pinpoint the exact moment it happened and I wish I could change it. Alas life is raw and sometimes the burns last.-

Fire away in rapid succession
but
you are too slow,
the virus takes over,
Claiming cell after cell until one is crippled.
Flooding your veins with poison,
as years unfurl.

Hang on,
Even though your heart wishes to let go

Waiting

Awake for hours
I try to sleep
thoughts are everywhere,
I watch,
I cant help it
I am suddenly nervous,
Hands trembling
I need to wait,
wait and see

Room

Need room to breathe
can't shake the nerves
crawling up my spine
twitching back down my arms
everything will be ok, right?

Demons

The day is young
I am satisfied, literally
Chase the dragon
dry out
Ideas flood my brain,
I struggle
I swallow my nerves,
my thoughts
Being with her is dangerous to my psyche,
more so than I am willing to admit

Shame

The mere thought
illuminates too many questions
Vanilla fills the air,
Stopping just long enough
to coat the creases of my neck

GMC

I have just emerged from a circle
of GMC goodness,
foggy,
I need to gather,
Smoke still pulsating through my limbs.
Senses amplified
I think about her,
I breathe in deeply,
Vanilla & summer with a hint of coconut
I need her to back down

Secrets

-Everyone has them. Some acknowledge that they are there, others
just forget about them or try to ignore them. How about you?-

A woman waits for the sun to rise,
when answers appear and all else is lost

Wind sweeps in and shifts the pain of the past
leaving a void, scrutiny,
inviting tighter security, accepting the knowledge of fate come to
terms

The Earth will swallow your secrets
 and bury them so no one will ever know,
yet the hidden seeds blossom and bear fruit.
They grow, stronger and taller each year,
a reminder of what once was,
the past haunting and plaguing your dreams.

When the fire comes to burn away the memories,
You will find comfort in the torment of your own thoughts.
Raging, it will bring peace and tranquility,
awaiting
death.

But the secrets shall remain,
buried deep within the earth, untouched,
waiting for the chance to blossom again.
She will not die, but merely await
a time,
a time when the tractors arrive
to
tend the withered crop.
Leaving her to live in terror,
waiting for the cleansing rain that will never come,
an old woman, blinded with the elements of a secret,
cruel, unchanging, dark.
An old woman, waiting for the sun to rise,
forever afraid to dream.

Cheerleader

-If you wait too long you miss your chance to act. I most certainly
did.-

What thought did I provoke?
What media did I stir up?
My memories serve no purpose for you,
so why should I damage you with them?

The pursuit of deliverance avenges a lust,
spoiled and sticky from the mouth of a drug;
A rainmaker is who you are,
lost in the satin sheets I laid out for you.

Whatever makes the days stop is what I relish for.
The missed frolics and battles between lovers
will be forgotten indefinitely.
Melancholic and uncurbed is the form I shall be taken by.
The world shall prey on my muted growl,
as vengeance is allowed to pour from the seams of my lining.

The roots of life shall be trampled
in the storm of a knife.
Shaky is all the wound shall be on the unshaven legs and tampered
with veins.
Images of my own funeral are kept at close length,
in front of all the cranial garbage,
a fixture of sorts to run from.
To partake in such an alluring obstacle,
frees the mind
from
its grief and misguided decisions.

2 Minutes 41 Seconds

-The memories will always be there, but some things are just not meant to be no matter how hard you manipulate the situation. You will miss what really matters if you aren't looking for the signs. Then again what is in front of you isn't always what you were hoping for.-

Push the limits
and
acknowledge
what is acceptable?
He is not,
she is not,
then who is????

The wall is pressing against my spine,
crushing what little is left.
My spirit is mean,
unable to balance tenderness with grief
angry at the notion,
I am alone.......yet all I can think of is you.
Fuck you!!!

Bitter to a fault,
it's my nature
and
your breath will get me no where.
I have wasted too much time,
chasing what you want.

I have circled the moon
and
peace is not within my grasp.
I call, vulnerable and diminished,
but
you are wrapped in your own cocoon,
aligned to another
and
unable to dry the tears I have summoned.

Do you really know me as well as you say?
Or
Have I been blinded by the scent of vanilla in the air?

Answer me damn it!
For your silence seems to prove what I have known all along.
That I was wrong,
misguided
and
drenched in the shadows of my own scathing misconduct.

I am unwilling to play the game,
your words twist the results
and
I am tired of losing to a less than formidable opponent.

I will always love you
even if you can't,
even if you won't,
even if you will never,
love
me
back.

7:00 AM

-Because anger is the easiest choice sometimes even if it isn't the right one.-

In the morning I was still, angry,
at you.
Imagine that, angry
at your presence,
your words,
your dedication to yourself.
Are you lonely yet?
You are my vindication,
the annihilation of thyne senses and a twisted sense of warmth.
I am cold, cold in your world
and yet you do not see me shivering.
You are contagious,
weak
and
your walls seem to be crumbling in my hands.
We are drowning, a blood bath, drawn by me,
competing, thriving, sidestepping
to appear stronger.
Or is it all for nothing?
I have already won, you just don't know it yet.
The phoenix shall fly again, free from ash,
ready to feast on your words.
I love you too......

Who calls this early anyway?

Family Secrets

-The secrets they lay tucked away, behind a door that you will not
find. Behind that door is where the truth resides. Do you embrace it
or let it frolic past you?-

I opened my eyes today
to find that you were not there.
A cool whisper set in
and wrestled with my skin,
while unwanted tears attacked.
The echoes are louder in the morning,
as the heart undresses for the day,
dark, open and unattended
but for the love of a butterfly.

Beyond the span of her wings there is no light,
No trees for shelter,
No flowers for fragrance,
No cocoons for protection,
Inside and quiet, I must simply wait
for her.

Date the picture wrapping your brain,
the last curve of her face as you brushed against her lips.
Say goodbye for a time, tentatively.
Can you see
which direction her hair fluttered,
what color her eyes were
and exactly when she let go of your hand?
Paint it, relive the grace of her touch,
holding on just tight enough to say,
I love you, don't leave,
but loose enough to slip away in the breeze.

Brown Eyes

- How ironic….. I find truth in these words and know the pain that comes from their recitation but don't believe that they will ever make the anger subside. I love my friends dearly and with that comes the knowledge of their flaws, both fatal and nagging, and I must create an existence where I don't pay attention to any of that only I don't know if I can. I shall wait and see.-

When I see
YOU
dressed like a queen, prancing in a parade of onlookers
I am ill
Too haughty to notice or catch my small wave
You ignore me

In your spring Prada pumps, jonesing for a high class man
I pity you
Burning your bridges, leaving friends out to dry
Who are you?

We used to be sisters-strong, elite, together,
unphased by the way word upper class.
Your hair is light, your eyes immune
I am sad for you
Hunting for a precocious white knight,
He does not exist
He will be plagued by your mind-distraught and misshapen -of your
own accord
Am I mistaken?

Platinum and ice, is your prize
Left scorched by the grit of your dragon
At your wedding I toast your love,
Sing praises, dance with pride, build a wall for redemption
and we perish
as
I
stand up
to
leave

Lost

She stops to feel my pulse,
it races faster, the longer she lingers
Uncomfortable,
I push away
Up the nape,
just enough to leave and impression,
whispering something I can't remember

7:30 PM

She smells amazing,
Always does,
JD lingers,
you want she asks?
Yes, I think to myself,
but all I can manage is
no

2001

Interruptions are everywhere,
Mom, friends, cousins,
Unavoidable
All I can think about is the yellow submarine,
processing will have to wait, I suppose
Sneaking around
excites me under the surface
How am I supposed to go back now?
She isn't right,
I release her,
we part, my heart wants

A Girl

She stops me with an abrupt yank,
I freeze,
Hours pull me,
I want to say something, but my words escape me,
I can't be
I can't be
I can't be,
I will not allow it,
It's not a good idea,
I can't love this girl, she will break me

Anxiety

Everything crowding my brain halts,
Then melts away,
Impatient,
Working,
Reaching,
Trying to stifle it all
I emerge and crash
I can't figure out what I want
Too bad it's all for naught

Lost in the Ashes
-Very early in the AM-

What's left to possess?
Roses, sheets, sweaters, a stale bag of chips,
There are too many exasperations,
Neighbors for life, vanishing in a flicker

Exhausted by the flight,
Flowers to seed and back again,
Thread the places around me,
For on a string they can never be lost

I drank for you today,
an a bit for myself.
The puddles have grown since you left,
New faces made from sparkling play dough
You might be laughing,
I shall not though,
For the drop that remains is smaller than ever

She is like me, with love,
Give it to those who are deserving, fuck the rest
The trail is incinerating in front and all around,
Days move forward,
Nights fall back,
Hang on for me,
I will lend you my hand,
so morning can us find,
in the same place-across the bridge

You Look so Fine

Follow the threads,
Crumbs leading you down a path,
It will not be like this forever,
this path is unstable

Cruelty is gentle in the eyes of loss,
but who smeared the ink?

Right,
I did

Fall into the place that drew the picture,
Memories are my savior,
Without them the present becomes a figment,
A shard at the foot of the dragon
who's flames you are still cursing

You are near, just beyond my grasp,
I call but you can not speak,
I shudder but you can not feel,
I cry but you can not see

The world is still, but for me
A rush to smother the solitude looms near

Visions

-Sometimes remembering is harder than you think-

It's been too long, and I am having trouble remembering,
your face

I never imagined being here,
alone and
in a foreign pasture, filled with cackling hyenas
Can you hear it from there?
I am trying to ignore it, but
I can't....
Standing amongst them, I need to disappear
and soften the rope as it tears through the wall I seem to be standing
on.....

What exactly are they doing here?

Step back and ignore the uneasiness,
it shall pass in the frolic of the moment
Envision her hand,
pressed, gently on your chest to feel the beat underneath
She is smiling as you reach for hers,
but you are startled by a voice, and then, she is gone
in a chattery wisp of salt water breeze,
and
you are here again, with them,
nibbling away at the pebbles crumbling about their feet.
A hand reaches towards you, urging you to join the circus,
Can you trust???
The message is mixed, but belief is drawing you in.
Try and resist, bound by the life left behind,
After all being in love is breathless, even in its true ugliness.

These are the Moments
-Sometimes a revision is necessary-

I opened my eyes to find
that you were not there,
Wrestle with the itch resting beneath the skin,
While unneeded tears attack my breathe

The echoes are louder in the morning,
As my heart undresses for the day,
Dark,
Open
And
Unattended

Date the picture wrapping your brain,
As Eileen did, for posterity
The last curve of a face,
saying goodbye for the moment

Can you see?
Which direction her hair fluttered,
what color her tank was,
and when exactly she let go of your hand
Fingertips, just tight enough to say, I love you,
loose enough to skip away in the mist of the day

Listening

#13

Am I being too slow for you?
I banter
No, you are overthinking,
I see it in your eyes
Let it go, she demands, settle
Lines blur,
Innocent victims to my desire
Anger and frustration flood the veins,
she twirls,
I twirl,
That's my girl, she whispers,
there is nothing to unravel over
but she is wrong

#14

-Same time, same day, same year-
Sitting back,
She slips free,
A fire that burns,
Nails graze,
Impatience,
I love it, for the moment,
Until the pressure explodes
The ringing begins,
Quiet I say, pressing the talk button,
The conversation is short,
I slam the phone,
I told you not to answer it she laughs

#15

Sometimes those we love, push just a bit too hard
I am not
So stop telling me that I am
I am not
Fine, you aren't now
 but you were then and that terrifies you

Tears fall,
One
Two,
three,
 too many to count

Yes

Yes what?

Yes, I was,
are you satisfied?
I tried to ignore it, but I couldn't
that just made it worse,
so
much
worse

#16

-The first time I ever went to therapy, I cried the whole time.
Then I promptly found another therapist-

Have you sent it yet? She demands
No, I have not

Why?

I don't know, I really don't know
I just can't bring myself to do it

Are you afraid that you need her?

Grow up,
You do need her

#17

-Therapy was not my friend early on, not at all-

What is the end game here?
Do you have one?

No

That is crap, I know you do
What is the end game?

My puzzle is missing a piece

Then find it

#18

-She says it like it's so easy-

I made choices,
had feelings,
Life had other plans, things played out differently

Have a discussion?
Its sounds so simple,
A discussion could make things uncomfortable
I don't want to look into the past,
I want to move on,
Gain
Peace and closure

Not all things are meant to be said,
Saying them now,
She doesn't need to know,
I don't need anyone to know

Once I say it,
It will always be out there
I know her,
She doesn't need to know I am broken

Impasse

-I can't shake this song I heard on One Tree Hill, it's about God,
how ironic. I imagine when I walk through my own valley of
death that I will be at peace and that what I have written here will
be the last thing on my mind. -

At my feet they rest, puddles
Two, three, ten – the number is of no consequence.
Sticky,
bubbling to a gentle boil
one limb at a time, staining the skin
climbing, stealing the sentiment, I have to let it go?
I resist, crying out, grieving.
The battle surging, devouring the remnants of my amicable
nature.

I can't get it off, the fire,
Branded by my own creation.
I can't swallow, scalded into submission.

The rationale
has
dissipated,
rippling and piercing as it blazes around me, growing,
choking the oxygen that remains.

Who am I?
Please give rest to thy soul –

I am struggling for more time – writhing in the contamination,
I have abandoned the idea of true hope,
drowning,
gasping for every breath
as the vengeance
explodes, searing all that is
left,

anger

In Remembrance of Summer

Waves, that's all that they are,
waves of thought and only seconds to catch them.
Hurry or they shall pass as they often do, because I am not eager
enough to write them.
But dreams they hold so much intrigue and wonder that I can't help
but write this one down as it passes.

Summer Lightening

Motion through the night,
Pulsing slow, all around me,
beating under my skin
and in my veins,
Wake from the lightening, electric, in its thoughts,
But warm in its light.
Hiding carelessly behind the heat,
On an aimless journey
across the sky,
Go
ahead
look
for it,
You'll find it
Just outside the window

Eyes

I thought of her last, when she wasn't around. I couldn't help it,
I wished she was there.
I bet that would scare her, I know it scares me.
It's the way she hangs on, close,
Tight.
You don't want to let go, but you do, worried that she will
sense.....
I wish I could mask the quivers I get when she is near,
But
What would be the point, hiding just increases the longing
I miss her face

Cumulus Turmoil

-I remember the last time I was here, and I seemed to have blocked the memory. How is it that I have allowed things to reach such an uncontrolled point. I mean it's not as if the words haven't been there to say, I have just been selfish. I can hold my own, except I haven't been. I am afraid of what is coming and of what could happen. I don't know what is in store, but I laugh at the irony of my situation.-

White flames of summer
adrift in a waltz of blue
and
left to simmer in the breeze

Wisps and strands
patiently cascade the spine of a dreamer,
entranced
by far off tremors of possibility, to which
I am deeply aware

Wait and be still,
lingering too long in the whistle of dragons and castles,
clenching
the first loss of my female form,
to which I am savagely fearful

Inhale the crimson fumes
and collapse under the tension,
All eyes are at rest, your screams
sequestering in the cruelty of circumstance,

to which I shall stand shivering,
alone and profoundly
Awake

A City Unknown

-The place this comes from is gone, but I have stolen the feelings
needed to make it happen-

Fizzle,
Splutter, gasping for air.
A single breath
shall ignite the flame,
lying
in
wait.
Breathe too strong and the fire will rage,
not enough breath and the embers will burst
just before
collapsing.

Glow,
Grow,
Rest,
Warming the memories,
Savoring the moments,
Guarding the door.
The door from which I shall wait,
for the embers,
to choose the path
they
will
follow

Inside Out
-A Tribute to my Fellows-

Held tight by its sheath
it exists, if only in the mind of one

Jeweled and disdainful it stands,
a champion of neglected verse
whimpering,
for I am still wary

Raging near and unphased- it hungers – for freedom,
seeking doers of justice and all keepers of pain

I admire its prowess, sharpened by a miscalculation of senses
A mistake of emotion fills the air, clearing away certainty,
replacing each breath with a gasp
Take it in-we are all the same-varied only by our seeing

The heart is killed by love and betrayal cheats itself,
 leaving time to make up the difference
I am no longer wary

Reflections of the self, burst forth from the shadows,
misguided,
regretful
and
flooded in form

We hold on
The murmurs are near, resonating, facilitating
and
growing in power,
I am no longer wary

Pleas of lost memories vacate the barren scene and we are here
 left alone in our molds of the past
Bearing weapons
- we are strong-
seeking answers to bandage the fragments
They are powerful in their truth
 still
 bleeding from the swipe our swords

The Conversation

Making amends,
it is an intimate thing.
It is delicate and uncharted but it is part of growing
I cannot ignore it.
I cant change without accepting who I once was
I cant grow without seeing who I want to be
I don't know that I am pleased with all of my choices,
but they are mine
Have you made amends with your past?

The Conversation – Part 2

How does one begin again?
The years have trickled by silently
with no words to remember them by,
only conversations, visions, fantasies and what-ifs.
The pieces are laid out- scattered.
The picture will begin to form with time,
Shaping the memories I have hidden
in an effort to move forward and climb.

Atop the skyline I feel them,
clawing at my interior.
The story must be told - if only for my own gluttony.
Eat away and swallow the sting,
as her memory tingles the skin,
pushing its way to the surface.

Have you let go yet?

Peach Cobbler

-It's becoming easier again, to place the words. They creep in when I am showering or cooking dinner. I don't know if its the buzz of summer in my ear, but I am happy. I am writing and that is all that matters, at least that is what my friend told me. She said just write and the rest will finds its way. I believed her, if only I knew then what I know now….-

A pretentious **Sunday morning**-to revel in thought,
nestled   away
in the swollen lips of **Savannah.**
The air is tight , unforgiving,
and
dripping with the stains of summer.

Hours amble past, finding pleasure in the fury
of an aged country inn
Sweet tea
One lemon
and a porch cloaked in haze-**Is it August already?**
Raise an eye to the warmth, bathing tourists and fellows.
Still.
Copper kettles
and
wooden planters, brewing treasure in their wake-
Do you garden?

Overgrown and unkempt,
chattering blossoms
distract a tiny child,
painting her tongue with blueberries.

Shutters tapping-don't be startled

the day is breathing, splintered
and
hinting of **orange –n- honey**
I have rested-filling pages, emptying hearts-
come join me

I saved a seat for you

Riverview **Women**

-Mom is upstairs being put back together and I am watching the boats
pass to stay calm. Sitting at a corner table in the Dunkin Donuts are
two women having a very deep discussion. Their words sadden and
comfort me all in the same breath.-

Count the vessels as they pass
One, two, three, four,
Tinkering in the breeze,
meandering,
combing,
searching.
Will they find the passage they are looking for?

Nearby the discussion is loud,
profound
and
hard to avoid.
Two women,
agreeing and disagreeing between the laughter.
They speak of love,
their fear of sharing it
and the pain of receiving it or worse being denied.
One will not say the words even if she means it,
The other states it too often
and
finds her life filled with regrets.
Rejection

and
Reciprocation,
working hand in hand has branded them both in different
ways.
How ironic?

I want to walk away,
return to the floor from which I came,
but I am compelled,
their words ring too close.

The effort to press on,
disappointed in their choices or lack thereof,
it saddens me.
How long has it been since you have said, "I love you?"
One day,
One week,
One month,
One year.
The greater the span the stronger the need.
Giving love freely is a choice,
that takes work.
Are you prepared for what could be discovered?

You say I love you,
but do you mean it?
Have you ever meant it?
Are you offended by my words?
I personally resent the idea of their words,
The negatively is clouding the serenity around me,
yet I cannot bring myself to leave them.

Make a choice,
a choice to accept who you are,
who you once were
and who will be.
We are all humans,
humans that must choose to love,
because waiting for it
might cost you your entire life.

Truest Form

-Bold and Unyielding Towards Only Myself-

Words, words, words.....oh where did they come from????

Hidden for some time,
I guess the proper encouragement was necessary,
but has it really arrived?
I feel more blessed than ever before, yet I am torn by a growing
sorrow,
the pains of a life changing moment.
I shall just to push it aside....
time cannot erase all things ,
yet,
can the heart ever be brave enough
to reveal its purest, most intense passions
without being asked?

Hunger

Stare and
 wait, for the sun, to whisper
 me the palest breeze

Caress your face, as it passes,
Gathering only, a few breaths,
of what is available
before vanquishing

Walk on,
until the rhythm, of your feet, begins to fade.
Settle in and reside within the function of your own visions,
The words, etched ceremoniously,
billow about a borrowed ear

Ache behind the crisp silence, mourning.
Unrelenting, the search for a trusting hand,
Remaining constantly true to form and
Unwilling to let go

Simmer in the writhing afterglow,
of nightmares, waging war,
upon your solace,
and choking the flowers hungry for more

Scream out
alone,
in the dark,

as if she is hidden, behind the angels of the night.
Stay with me
or else - I shall lie awake, and stare,
waiting for the sun
to take away the uncertainties, pent up and aged,
to close out the evening

Heather Sawyer

Can you hear me?

Hello

-I can't shake the dream. Every night, going on six months,
I am wondering if it will ever cease. Maybe I don't want it
to???-

The repetition is scorching,
blazing the interior
rerouted
to the heart.
The thoughts permeate the outer core,
flooding the nerves with each new image.

Drown in perspiration, feeling each scene as it passes.
She is there, hold her hand, breathe in softly.
There is a hint of vanilla drifting
in front of the consequences,
waiting to be tasted.

Ravage the distance,
blinded by boundaries,
one hurtle at a time.
Her palms are warm with duress,
curl up inside
and
wither in peace.

The room is dark
and
you are not alone.

Occupied with your own prehistory,
sleep escapes down the stairs,
wrestling to forgive
the misconception of the scented flame
left burning in the kitchen.

Sensitivity

For Her

-In the aftermath of the previous days I am struggling to figure things out. What is it that I am terrified of?? I am not sure that I know, but when I am alone it creeps in, trying to warn me to stop.-

Slam into the reins of the Calypso Palace,
daunting lights and horrific smoke.
Dance as the floor seeps in beneath you.
Recover and form a direction.
What am I doing to myself?
Am I going somewhere behind these reins?

Remain clueless as the hints of starvation stagger in,
hunger for none other than the love I have chosen.
Fall into the cracks, I shall never,
but where is the strength?

The walls have opened,
smells slither in and misguided quandaries have
trampled past.
Two souls remain inside the fumes,
but the fire to have it all heightens the damage.
Pursue even when cautioned,
for a reason that I cannot answer:
Choke the thoughts for I am selfish within

and
I must silence the fever.
Allowing the sizzle to calm around her.
I am stubborn though
and
I shall flounder in a pool of myself.

Close my eyes
and
jump,
The ground is soft here
and
salvation is a tiny monster swiping at you morals.
If I duck,
I may find her standing there when I open my lids

Self - Concept

-Baby steps, they keep you moving forward most of the time.
Tonight I am the poster child for diminished self-concept. I
will not try again which is a shame really. Thousands of tiny
steps eliminated in just under ten minutes time.-

At my feet they rest, puddles
Two, three, ten – no matter, they are one now,
sticky,
bubbling to a gentle boil
one limb at a time, enveloping the tenderness
climbing-stealing the passion, is it time?
I resist, crying out,
but I can't swallow,
I am scalded into submission.

The rationale has dissolved,
each ripple piercing as it simmers,
choking the heart of oxygen.
The chords are drowning,
fighting,
reaching,
gasping for every breath.
Is it time to leave?

Your voice is degrading,
Lies,
Do you hear yourself?
Impaled by your own lack of dignity,

I am broken.
I shall be mindful of my words
from here forward.

Best of luck finding me in the morning

Hidden

For my friend

—Do you ever wake up and wonder if you really are that
person staring back at you in the mirror? It's easy to
hide away from the world, I know she does. I think it
feels safe tucked away where no one can find her; but
that is what friends are for, to pull you back into the
sunlight.—

Shy away from the looking glass if you fear what lies
within,
there is truth to its reflection,
But at what cost?
Do you adore the figure you are gazing at
or
are you a work of fiction ,
drawn up to appease the world around you?

My hand is near to help you stand,
take hold.
I see you back there grappling for possession.
Don't back down, the world will forget what you allow.

The edges of your figure have grown dark,
shadows are hiding your face.
Open your eyes and look at me.
I see you.

What will it take to get **you** there?

Let the glass shatter,
You can rebuild, just believe.
I shall bleed for us both when the shards fall,
close your eyes and swing,
I will be right here next to you.
I see you······broken from time, damaged by words,
strangled by choices.
I see you
alone,
searching,
afraid.
I see you

Do you see anything besides yourself?

Did you ever see me?

Damaged

−It started with a conversation with an old friend and
ended with a weird dream. I believe I have reached my
breaking point for the moment. Time to get my shit
together and regroup.−

Close my eyes and swallow hard,
the words will disappear
at least for a time.
They shall never stay buried,
they are part of me, and so is she,
even if I do not want them to be.
Ignoring only increases the impact,
regardless of my lack of acceptance.
Do you see her?

She will be there, always,
because I want her to be.
Memories, daydreams, revelations,
tormenting my existence
and
impeding my growth.
Do you see her?

Depleted by circumstances of my own creation,
I will search for her, desperate and reckless,
fighting the need to the core.

Wedging the door open, if only for a second.
It will never be enough.
Do you see her?

Tired and broken, the lies build,
systematically diminishing what lays in front of me.
Digging deeper will not prove safe,
choking the innocent cannot vanquish the monsters.
Do you see her?

She is there, lingering
just
beneath
the
surface.
Aroused by my fears,
she is ready,
ready to capitalize
on the weakness that I allowed her to create.
Do you see her?

I wish I didn't

Boundaries

−I am restless and I don't like that. Restlessness leads
to trouble and I am no position to dig myself out of a
hole. She was right, I should listen to her more often.
The revelations come when you aren't looking for them.
I am learning to accept myself as I am. I am ok.−

Building walls is easy,
One brick at a time
Until you reach the desired height,
Just tall enough to see over, but too high to scale
Safety lingers between the cracks,
Salvaging the visions that remain

How fast you build is up to you,
but in time all will be blurred
and everything will be stained red.
You want to back away,
temptation is brushing against your cheek
and
the pull is growing too strong.

Tangled in a web of unjust circumstances
all of your own creation.
Coveting a life which
does not belong to you, it never will,
unless you reach for it.

Embrace the being you wish to unwrap, slowly,
admiring every inch of the surface.
Breath in the scent, of what could be
and what really is.
Years have passed,
but the ending has circled back.

Love,
tingling through your fingers,
electrifying the soul lost in the ashes.
Some boundaries are too great,
the fear of stretching across them lingers
behind you, always.
Do you even know what you want?

Afraid of what bubbles under the surface,
manipulated by perceptions,
the perception of others and the tainted perception of
yourself.
Ashamed of the desire lurking between the shadows,
even if it is what you truly want.
Can you live without it?
Because the tears will not hide forever,
and the urge will rise, devouring the soul
and
forcing your hand.
Your mask doesn't cover as much as you think,
she sees you, even if you don't want her to.

Unbridled pleasure,

imagined then cast aside,
victimized by the anxiety billowing
underneath.
Desire the dream
if only for a moment,
for
the demons will find you by daybreak
and she will be gone,
because
you are too afraid to
let
her
stay

A New Reality

-The dream has returned with a vengeance. A week
had passed and nothing, I was psyched, only for it to
reoccur twice in one night.-

Belief in the unknown will follow you in circles,
Whimpering and waiting for the answer to come.
Do you have it?
Scamper, shuffle, and dodge the rings,
It will keep up.
Learn from it, ignore it, the choice is yours.
Dizziness will set in eventually,
rendering what remains.
Belief,
scalded with useless words.
I believe in you,
Without strings,
Without reciprocation,
Without acknowledgement,
I believe in you.
What for, I do not know.
My actions are blinded and senseless,
beyond the bubble of view,
do you even want to be my friend?

I am starting to question everything,
and
I always end up

with
unintended consequences.
The anger always leads to them,
the question is, how do you get away from them?
They follow you, just as belief does
and
often lead to one another
Jumbling together the memories that remain.
I want to feel them and move along,
but
are
they
worth
acknowledging?

To do that would mean conceding,
a loss of the last bit of belief
In myself.
What shall remain, I cannot say,
a mere shadow in the glow
of what once stood tall.
Belief
I had it once,
before I surrendered to sweet scents of summer.

Belief
I had it once,
before,
before I,
before I let her in.

Underdog

–It's hard to understand why I have such a need for acknowledgement. I lived without it for so long, but I almost wonder if that makes it worse. I need to relax and let go because the core of a person never truly changes and if I ever want to feel complete I need to just accept that.–

Push away the victims lost in their own revelry.
I cant breathe under your stare.
I am drowning,
attached to something that simply does not exist.
My words have crushed the resurrection, I knew they would.
Love
muddles the contact
and
starves the effort to move forward
if it is not reciprocated.

Come close, please,
don't make me beg.
The need is too great and I am crippled by it.
Why do I love you?
Have you ever really loved me?
I am starting to doubt my own reality

I have a little life in me yet,
scratching to find the surface, without you
because you were never really here to begin with.
Give me every moment back,
so much time – lost.
The things we did
and
the ones we missed.

I wish I could just make it all go away,
but the circle always whips back around,
blistering the skin with each new bite.
The vision is never the reality,
but the belief keeps me waiting,
Waiting for you to
make a move,
any move,
first.

Girlhood Dreams

-The snow is swirling and I am cleaning, sorting, and remembering the past. The days when things were simple and you answered the phone when people called.-

Previously, it was the fear of uncertainty.
Presently, it is the fear of certainty,
of consistency,
of routine,
of knowing where to go and what to do.

A hesitant push to return to a life, forgotten,
a life which is desperately trying to be molded
by a society not believed in.
Regret at the possibility of being forced to be a version
of a self
which does not exist.

A threat - a threat to life itself;
a threat to love,
a threat to a love of life,
so easily obtained
and
more easily discarded.

A struggle to retain,
all that has been gained,
pleasure.

Pleasure in knowing,
that success is easily within my grasp.

Her Words-Not Mine

-A circular motion is not always what is needed-

You don't leave,
You don't hurt me,
You see what I don't see
Around you,
I am me,
I am happy

I would rather be with you
than
anyone else

When I am alone,
I am tempted,
I wander,
I get lost,
I am not me

After

−I despise therapy at times, because I don't like to see
what she sees. Sometimes I don't want to go, but I
know it helps. I also know she is right more often than
not−

I catch her smile
out of the corner of my eye,
I want to know what she is thinking,
I hold back.

My vulnerability
is unmatched with her,
I hate that.
She creates doubt
and
weakness.

Yet I follow the aroma blindly,
for in the morning things will
L
O
O
K
different

Neon Lights

-Screw Pandora, I will find something better-

I
saw
the
flashing
red
lights

They were hard to miss

I
saw
them
clearly

I simply chose to ignore them

and

peer
inside
anyway

The Details

I came with nothing,
I will leave with nothing

simple

unless, you consider resentment

something

Grace

-One hug at a time please-

I have boundary issues,
serious boundary issues,
don't touch my arm,
don't rub my leg,
don't hold my hand
and
don't even think about hugging me

Weird,
I am aware,
try talking to me while I am
in
the
tub

Me

-Accept who you are, she tells me. What if I don't want
to? What do I do then?-

I don't let people in,
only once in a while,
I don't cry in public,
I don't call all the time,
I don't do blood
&
I will not pick up after the dogs, ever

I love long, super-hot showers,
I write notes everywhere,
then loose them,
I take pictures all the time, nature most of all,
I savor memories and dwell on missteps

I am loud, way too loud,
but I don't care
I am an organized disaster at times,
I thrive in chaos
I talk A LOT,
non-stop,
those who know me best just tell me to shut it

I don't sing and I most definitely do not dance
I get angry easily
and

I love to a fault

I don't swim,
I refuse to wear swimsuits in front of skinny people
and
I especially don't go to public pools,
I find them revolting
Amusement parks make my skin crawl,
But I could sit under a covered bridge for hours

I love the American Revolution
&
I loathe the Civil War.

I am a complete word nerd
but I don't tell people that
I can cook,
I can write
&
I can teach
I cannot talk in front of huge groups

I will swallow my pride when necessary,
but I might hold a grudge
I am a jealous person,
who worries about others opinions

This is me

Kingsley

-Architecture in AP-

Right, left,
Right, left,
One block at a time,

Stop to admire,
The red door calling your name,
Fill your brain with the image,
Up,
Up,
Up
You will climb

Stairs to Heaven?
Stairs to nowhere?
Stairs to Hell?

Climb until your gait is woozy
and
the breeze chills your being

Try and not walk too high,
you may tip your hand
and spoil the view

Moss

-Have you killed a plant lately?-

Grass,
Children,
Flowers,
Animals,
Crystals,
Hair,
Waist lines,
Skills,
Lies,
Depression,
Fear,
Love,
Hatred,
Confusion,

all take time to grow.

Lost Copper

−Around and around they go, where they go, only they
can know−

Two loops,
24 samples,
58 degrees,
Salt water as far
d
o
w
n
as
Toast

broken bricks,
sentenced to a new beginning,
under the arches, boards stretch,
reaching for the waves of color billowing
against the wall

W

−Dark roast, flavored, iced, it doesn't really matter, it helps me to talk. I think it gives me something to fidget and deflect with, but I shall not dwell on the why.−

I brought coffee,
Can we sit for a while?

Why does the couch feel so far away today?

Notes from the Phone

−I write them, then I revisit them, again and again. I
think it's time to delete a few−

I don't want to be you,
I don't want to be you,
I don't want to be you,

but

I am you
and
I am resentful that you get to be me

Can You Hear Me Yet?

I am not a horse
and
I do not like water

I cannot be made to drink

However
find me a bovine and I could be persuaded

Egg Whites & Cheese

-Changing my view one sandwich at a time-

Rituals,
they keep me grounded and still.
I can focus
when I can see what is coming.

Control,
I don't have it,
my head thinks I do

The couch is safe,
covered in pillows to catch me
if my vulnerability begins to show.

Galaxy Drive

-It always comes back to her, no matter how much I try
and shake her off-

Diabolic snow chasms
whip through a tightly wound room
No warning, as before,
Upon us it shall remain

Solace is found
In snow angels,
Flying ice balls,
Petty shovelers
and weary children sledding

Dance in the drifts,
Search for the childhood coat and mittens
Later

I digress at the bitterness of men
made from ice and sticks,
Grandpa is smoking their pipe, this moment
In the window seat snow thrives in

Statue in the Rough

She mumbles something,
that is too flat to decipher,
The sky has deleted her on purpose,
so she goes
To cry means to let the world wake before her,
yet to sleep might mean getting passed over

Paper Boxes

A little girl,
Living inside a box on the corner of Avenue A,
People pass her by and stare- like she is a circus act,
She merely glares back and laughs

Tiny paper cuts outs they are,
All linked by the hand,
Easily torn and quickly trampled by the wind

How silly these people look,
construction paper dolls
with drawn on emotions

Wish I didn't need them so much, she thought

About the Author

I write, I teach, I mother, I LOVE Donuts and I live in the great state of NJ. I don't believe there is anything else pertinent to this story.

Can You Hear Me?

www.ingramcontent.com/pod-product-compliance
Lightning Source LLC
Chambersburg PA
CBHW071926020426
42331CB00010B/2738